The Rose Thorn's Purpose

Asia Marie Jackson

AFFLATUS PRESS PUBLISHING
Thousand Oaks, CA 91359
www.afflatuspresspublishing.webnode.com

The Rose Thorn's Purpose
By Asia Marie Jackson

Copyright © 2011-2012 Asia Marie Jackson
ALL RIGHTS RESERVED

First Printing - July 2012
ISBN: 978-0-9857437-1-0

NO PART OF THIS BOOK MAY BE REPRODUCED IN
ANY FORM, BY PHOTOCOPYING OR BY ANY
ELECTRONIC OR MECHANICAL MEANS, INCLUDING
INFORMATION STORAGE OR RETRIEVAL SYSTEMS,
WITHOUT PERMISSION
IN WRITING FROM THE COPYRIGHT
OWNER/AUTHOR

Printed in the U.S.A.

SPECIAL THANKS TO ALL THOSE THAT
HAVE AND CONTINUE TO INFLUENCE,
EMPOWER, AND INSPIRE MY LIFE.

CONTENT

The Rose Thorns Purpose	12
Understanding	13
Branch Of Knowledge	14
Love Is	15
U·N·I	16
For Always	17
Pure Love	18
God	19
One 2 Grow On	20
Grow on Love	21
Destiny	22
Conscience Smitten	23
Exercise Your Love	24
Muse	25
Nature Is One of Awe	26
Forward Movement	27
Salute	28
Reflexion	29
Backbone	30
Memories Of Season	32
Under The August Moon	34
Eventually	35
Ebony Splendor	36
Love Can Endure Strong	38
Life Secrets	39
Your Temple	40

Limitations	41
Give. Give. Give.	42
Giving Back	44
Down To Business	45
Silence	46
Seducing Silences	47
Equilibrium	48
Consecrate	49
Eternal Love supply	50
Cherish What Can't Be replaced	52
Equality	53
Grateful	54
Religion	56
Adore	57
Carbonado	58
B.l.a.c.k.	60
Sistah Girl In Italy	61
Mind Your Mouth	62
Proverbs: 18:8	63
Who Are You Calling Crazy?	64
Forgiveness	65
Asia	66
Do Your Homework	68
Lemons	69
Be Positive	70
Vohu Manah	71
Tonka	72
To Know His Music Is To Know Him	74
11.26	75

The sacred Trinity	76
Remain In faith	77
When Situations Arises	78
It's Sort Of Funny, Yet Kind Of Sad	79
Stop The Violence	80
This Indian Girl	81
All Seasons Long	82
Let's Plant Them & Watch Them Grow	83
Triumphant Thursday	84
Be Accountable	85
Do It For Yourself	86
Eureka	87
Zaggin	88
Humility	90
So Simple Then	91
Thousand Oaks Morning	92
The Bigger Person	93
Reflection	94
Enlighteners	95
Yes It Is	96
Worth A Thousand Words	97
It Is The Best Policy	98
Bid Farewell	99
The Human Brain	100
Clarity	101
Elemental Love	102
Earth	104
With(in) you	105
Come Build With The Queen	106

Gratitude	108
Get Thee Behind Me	109
What Once Was Will Be	110
A Soul Mate Encounter	112
He Makes Time	113
Carefully Chosen Words	114
Who's Counting?	115
I Want To	116
Stepping Stone	117
Reflections Of True Self	118
7	119
Tales of an Urban Sufi	120
Respect	121
No Rush	122
Orange Arie	123
Babies	124
Splendiferous Sunday	125
Set The Example	126
Surmount	127
Happiness Is Here	128
Enjoying The Tweets & Tapping Sounds	130
The Deadliest Weapon	131
Submission Takes Humility	132
Casual Sex	133
Asia	134
Forgive Me	135
Kiss	136
The Shape Of Beauty	137
Low Clouds	138

Messy People	139
Braggart	140
Read More	141
Oak Trees	142
Autumn	143
Eden	144
Pathfinder	145
Better Than They Imagine	146
Visions	148
Sharing Is Caring	149
Communication	150
Evermore	151
Beauty	152
Uplift	153
Fifth Commandment	154
Poetry To Me	155
Sterns Wharf	156
Maximal	158
Giver Of Kingship	159
Magnificent Yellow	160
Birds	161
Power Of Poetry	162
I Write	163
Perennial	164
ENCORE:	
Rain	167
Black Mother	169
God Made Me Free	174

Acknowledgements

I offer heartfelt thanks to the following people:
My mother Oranjarie Brown for her contribution of three poems and for her love and support;
To my editor Tony Seybert for his clear eyes and ever-judicious guidance;
To Kenneth D. Andrews Jr. for his devotion and creative graphic designs;
To my family and friends that provided advice and resounding cheers along the way;
And, lastly to you the reader for your constant support, motivation and encouragement.

The Rose Thorn's Purpose

POETIC EXPRESSIONS
ASIA MARIE JACKSON

Cover design by: Kenneth D. Andrews Jr.

The Rose Thorn's Purpose

Do not try to break me for being beautiful
The rose thorns within me rise
Like horripilations all over my body
I am protected by nature.
Do not try to obtain me for being exotic
My rose hips, enthralling fragrance
And ancient shaped petal lips
Is the passion for procreating.
Love me for what my roots have produced
As seasons transform
I will continue to be strong
With a contagious smile.
So while
You're in my presence
You smile and generally feel good
About yourself, love and life.

Understanding

A combination of

Knowledge and wisdom

Incorporated with

Comprehension, discernment and empathy.

Branch Of Knowledge

It takes a spiritual and disciplined ability to be in the world but not of the world. To be an illuminating, loving and peace courier of our beloved Father in this earthy world, one must bide in equilibrium in all situations and at all times. One must be loving and speak with healing words.

It takes a spiritual and disciplined ability to remain unswayed by the temptations, illusions and temporary pleasures of life, and to not be driven by fear, fame or sex.

It takes a spiritual and disciplined ability to remain even-tempered, when right or wrong, in victory or loss, with praise or criticism, in pleasure or pain and in sickness or health.

It takes a spiritual and disciplined ability to be involved with life, be in this world, and yet remain unaffected, therefore not allowing the world to get inside you.

Love Is

To commit yourself without warranty,
in hopes that your love will rouse love in your loved ones.

U·N·I

Like a pungi

My love plays a song of spirit

For you to hear its joy … and dance

Listen to my songs of soul

Hear its peaceful melody

Put your inhibitions on idle

And allow my heart's strings

To play its notes to you.

Quiet for a moment.

Allow me to hear the rhythm of your spirit

Now … that's peace.

We each have a song to share

Together we bring harmony to the universe

As we feel each vibration

Our energy brings songs

To the whole world around us.

It moves the cosmos and the stars around us

Your rays of light move this Earth

My Love allows you Sun to illuminate

Our Unity is the definition of Oneness.

For Always

I've been swept away to a place
Where your embrace
Is like a flood of sweet divine grace
There is love in you, in me, in we
Sacred alike the cycle of life
So this is where my destiny
Thought I ought to be
And I agree
In love and in truth
My-Self I share with you
And only you
The only thing I need
Is for you to NEVER let go

Pure Love

As Love fills my peace
I am reminded of whom I am
PURE LOVE
My physical body is filled with divine grace
Happiness gives me serenity with each sunrise
My path leads me to beautiful tomorrows
And my dreams do their best to come true

GOD

Gave everything in nature

PURPOSE

Including you!

One 2 Grow On

Sometimes the spiritual changes we make can cause us to lose friendships.

Some of our friends may be uncomfortable with us. Some may feel guilty about their digressions. Some may be unable to feel anything at all. Others may feel threatened by the changes we are making. If we find that friend or associate undermines our peace, we need to take caution of such relationships. This does not mean we do not reach out to unbelievers; it only means that we do not become too close to people who will lead us away from peace and truth.

Our primary relationships need to be with unselfish, godly people who will support our spiritual growth.

GROW ON LOVE

Love is life:

You feed it, you nourish it, and you cherish it with sincerity, purity and consistency. When you do not do these things, it gets malnourished; when you kill it, … it dies! May our living gardens remain filled with life, growth, beauty and love!

Destiny

When man meet woman
The connection is inevitable.

Conscience-Smitten

When she learned of his knowledge
She traveled very far … very far
Over land and sea
To learn from him.
When she had found him … indeed
His wisdom streamed upon her so suddenly
From his lips flowed the golden legend
Of the golden continent
His words were as revelations
Opening her eyes to visions of a new era
Cleansing her soul in showers of sunshine.
She communed with him of all that was
In her heart
He was smitten with her inner beauty
He saw her as a lily among thorns
Their love became the Song of Songs
The union of these two spiritual lights
Imbedded their combined wisdom and love
Into the DNA of the next generation.

Exercise Your Love

Your love will get stale if left on some dusty shelf in your mind. Take your love out for some fresh air by exercising your love on a daily basis. Love changes our attitudes from negative and weak to positive and powerful. When you live, think, breathe and see in love, everyone around you will feel your love and be inspired to love. Make love a part of your Self.

MUSE

You gave me inspiration to be me

To be free

To see all of God's people as royalty

In the Motherland

And as a matter of fact in America too

With our Africa and Indian blood

Yeah, we're all one

You gave me aspiration

To further my participation in this existence

And for you, I'll go the distance

You show me favor, mercy and grace

For this, I thank you

All praises due

Nature Is One of Awe

Whether one is feeling the heat from the Sun or rain upon ones head, or hearing the sounds of thunder, or picking fruit from a tree, walking a dog or hugging a cat, or enjoying the view from a mountaintop, planting seeds, feeding birds, walking on the beach or sailing the seas, the experience of nature is one of awe!

Forward Movement

It's a beautiful thing to realize

That you rule your destiny

Nature will take its course

Naturally, of course

But you have a say in your day's direction

With eyes wide open

Promote growth in life

With actions that gives inspiration

Some call it a blessing

Some call it direction

Some call it perfection

And others call it a lesson

If it's done out of love

I call it all of the above!

Don't give your first thought

A second thought!

Go with your instincts

And continue to live with days of enjoyment and fulfillment!

Salute

I uncork the bottle and pour my first toast and I raise high my glass
To the growth of our future from the strength of our past.
To the love and joy, that we feel and trust will grow.
To the taste of Moët and Chandon as I take my first sips.
To the taste of his lips and warmly said words.
To my heartbeat, that increases the pulse in my throat, when he holds me close.
To father time, that slowed down for us to enjoy this evening amid family, friends, love and laughs.
Salute!

Reflexion

My King doesn't define me

He refines me

Constantly reminding me of my strengths

He's not my lifeline

But he does keep my life in line

With truth and purpose

BACKBONE

My companion, lover and friend
Your light within radiates
From your inner spirit
Through your bronze skin
It is a blessing to be in a god's presence
Because there is something
So intoxicating and invigorating
About your very essence

Your eyes put me in a trance
You hypnotized me at first glance
Understand
It's more than just the physical
There's something about you
That have me so
Addicted to every bit of you

You're like a diamond
In its purest form
Before it starts changing
From its uncut and dark features

And some how society

Has this shadowy complex vision

Of you

But I am here

To let them know

You're so much more

You're a

Man

Father

Son

Brother

Friend

Lover

King

And the backbone of any community

Memories Of Season

A spring day I sat on the grass underneath cherry blossom trees at Lake Balboa Park. There were more butterflies than birds in the trees. These trees are testimonies to nature's beauty with their bright pink, white, green and brown hues. They truly are a complement to the lake.

A summer day I sat on top of a mountain in Wildwood Park in Thousand Oaks. There are hiking and bike trails and many cottontail rabbits hopping in the grass and shrubs. The view is so beautiful from up there. I like to go there to just breathe, relax and reflect on my blessings.

A winter night I looked out my French windows and watched and listened to the rainfall, I thought of having someone next to me to enjoy this peace and cup of hot tea but decided to enjoy the sight, the sound, the tea and my thoughts alone.

A fall afternoon my son and I took a boat ride on the Catalina Express to Catalina Island for lunch. We walked on the beach and got our feet wet and used sticks to write our names in the sand. Next, we took a stroll down one of Avalon's quaint Mediterranean-style streets and shopped for souvenirs. We ate at a beachfront restaurant where they served fresh seafood and broccoli the size of my son's head. Finally, we laid out on chaise lounge chairs on the deck outside the restaurant and talked about basketball.

Under the August Moon

Under the August moon
We viewed a loon as it swam into the wind
above the sea
Perfect scenery and symmetry
Just as we merged into one
It is such a beautiful sight to see your face
Under the August moonlight
Sharing this night with you
May we rest right tonight
And leave our body prints in the sand
Then bring home our fresh selves
And perhaps a rock and a couple of shells
To place in our home
As a reminder of how the sea tickled our toes
and dampened our clothes
As we made love
Under the August, moon
Where the twinkle in the sky matched the
twinkle in our eyes.

Eventually

As motions are to the ocean
So memories are to the mind
Moments come and evanesce
And if you remember, cherish and learn from them
You will forever be appreciative
Something then is left behind
A day, a moment, a time
To reminisce upon
Not for the eye to see
But for the heart to embrace
And when you stop questioning
Where all this is coming from
You will be ready to receive
Your eyes will open
As memories to the mind
And motions to the ocean
So love is to your soul
Eventually

Ebony Splendor

Quiet for a moment and listen
To the words of ancient songs
The pyramids stand on the land
Where the original man and woman stood proud, firm and strong
From the base to the tip all knowledge flows.
A King
A Queen
Great love unites a powerful force
Crossing over the sands of time
A whole new world by the Father's design
This planet third from the sun
Plays host to the children of God
The rising of the Sun in the east proclaims his presence.
And as we grow
And thrive
And multiply
Our passion beat like drums echoing along
The Nile

Joining heartbeats so strong the entire world could hear.

The words of wisdom
Are like pearls – hard to find
But once revealed – embraced
Like the unveiling of ebony splendor.

Love Endures Strong

Dubiousness … confines you in

Construct walls within

Do not allow fear to control you

Truth … sets you free

Live in reality

Enjoy the joy in living

Faith … uplifts you up

And if you have enough

You'll reach new beginnings

Love … endures strong

When you be it, live it, give it and receive it

You'll find the harmony in living

LIFE SECRETS

Are in roots

Roots of humanity and trees

Hidden deeply

Yet there to discover

Your Temple

Your physical body is the temple of your divine spirit. The truth is we are rapidly gaining weight. Our youth are in terrible shape. And being out of shape usually leads to all kinds of deficiencies, such as diabetes, lack of endurance and obesity. None of which will add years or quality to your life. Getting and staying healthy lies in the details of diet and exercise. Change won't happen overnight. The process may be tedious, but the results are well worth the effort. And not only will you feel better, you'll think and look better too! A sound body can enhance a sound mind. We may be spiritual beings, but while we're on earth our spirits are being housed in our physical bodies. Let's do everything we can to keep our temples in top shape.

LIMITATIONS

An ... Illusion

It's your own negative fear-based thinking that sabotages and limits you.

Give, Give, Give…

We have to start giving
We may think we don't have much to offer
But we've got a lot!
Let's give what we got
Give love, give time and give attention
Giving of ourselves is the most sincere and valuable gift we can give
Give of yourself, and everyone benefits

Give, Give, Give…
We have to start giving
Give encouragement, give patience and give understanding
The more you give of yourself, the more you find yourself
Give a hug, give a compliment and give a smile
Giving gives us a sense of empowerment and accomplishment

Give, Give, Give…
We have to start giving

We may think we don't have much to offer
But we've got a lot!
Lets give what we got
And what we got is worth much more than a gift wrapped in a pretty box!

GIVING BACK

Educating, tutoring, mentoring, feeding, loving, caring for, helping, listening to and talking with kids is my way of being obedient to the universal principles of service. Not to mention being an involved and present mother to my son. Being a single mother isn't always easy, but it is always my pleasure and my motivation for giving back!

Down To Business

I've heard this and I've heard that, but what is the end result? Talk huge and talk big on how you held your ground, but did you accomplish your goal? Did you get what you were trying to get or looking for? If not, you still have work to do and it may consist of you adding action to your words. Lose pride, lose fear and back your words up by being proactive and making a change.

Silence

The state of
The absence of
Sound
Exercise it sometimes!

Seducing Silences

My silence speaks volumes

Read my love written eyes

You know exactly how I'm feeling

No need to vocalize

The feeling that you give me

Words can't describe

Hear the pounds of my heartbeat

Let it wrap you all around

Its peaceful rhythm

Will submerge you

Into

My desire deep inside

Dare I reach out to touch you?

Do you think you'd realize,

How much I want you and need you?

You can see it in my eyes

I long to say I love you

Then embrace your reply

When I feel your lips on mine

I become paralyzed

In your seducing silence

EQUILIBRIUM

Silence filled the air so she walked toward the sound!

Consecrate

The Father Sun

The Mother Earth

The green pastures are the result

Of love, nourishment and commitment

To ourselves

To our descendants

And

To others

Eternal Love Supply

He is a god of chivalry

He wrote me love letters

He held my hand

While we danced on wilderness sand

In handmade linens

Embellished with turquoise, onyx and opals.

He is spiritual

He meditated

And ate the right foods

He is aware

He shared his knowledge with me

That was his way of protecting me.

He kept pictures of the Father

And African masks, literature and sculptures

As reminders of where he came from

Not that he had forgotten

But truth and righteousness

Became an often element.

He loves me

Not just because he told me

But how he showed me

He spoke to me
Sometimes in different tongues
English and Mathematically
He shared each sentence in good spirits
And each paragraph was but a meaningful moment in his presence.
His smile
Was peace dipped in beauty
His love came with no conditions
Only promises of an eternal supply.

Cherish What Can't Be Replaced

Give back to life

Seek, get and give knowledge.

See beyond the coat of flesh and the material

And get to the core

Focusing only on the outside

Is the quickest way to losing ones self.

Know thyself!

Equality

I urge you to come closer to me
And share with me the best I posses
And since this is about equality
I share with you – your best

Grateful

The truth-spoken beauty is rare indeed

He speaks with love

And leads with dignity.

He is cool

And

Tattooed

And

Intelligent

And

A little rough around the edges

And

All of that.

As a matter of fact

He is a rare find

Not only is he fine

He's kind

Kind to others, animals and our land.

He is the definition of a strong black man

He cooks and shares his life stories with me

He's giving of himself

Whenever there is a need

He is my friend that I can talk to

About any and everything.

He doesn't judge he listens

And gives his honest opinion

He is so accepting to life, nature

And the world we live in.

He gives a sense of closeness

Even when we are distant.

He is a man with a powerful journey

He inspires

To be in his presence is definitely valuable.

Even in silence I can hear his soul speak

He said as long as he has breath

I will never be lonely

He sees my true identity.

He welcomed me and gave me

The opportunity

To know him.

Religion

Separates us

We get so fixated on labels

We forget the content.

Give me the content

And you may keep the labels.

ADORE

The LOVE of my people

They can never take that away from me

I'll take that with me to the afterlife!

Carbonado

I shall call you Carbonado
You stand against fire and wind
A natural and priceless gem
A rock amongst men.

I shall call you Carbonado
You are brilliant
Your face reflects the Sun
Pure and sure
A source of warmth and energy
Your light shines from your heart
Illuminating the dark.
.

I shall call you Carbonado
Because of your fertile scintillating mind
You compete with no one
For you know there is no need
You are a rare and one of a kind gem
And a gift that I hold dear.

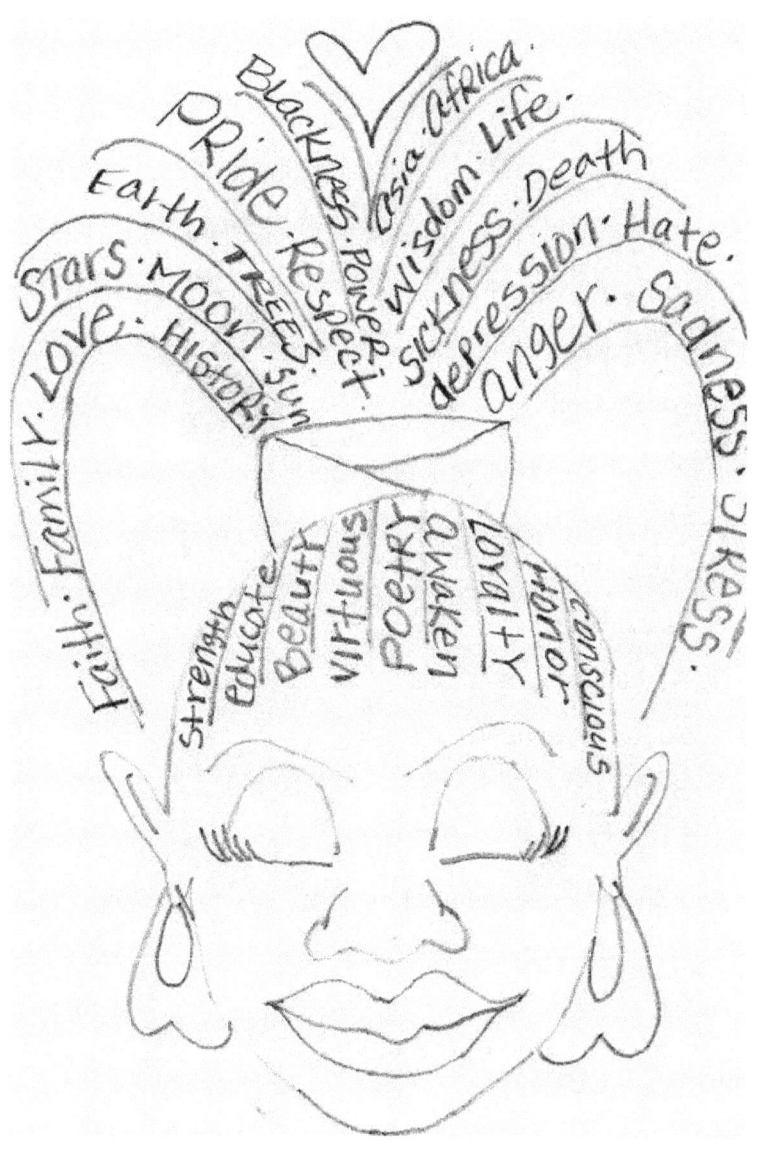

"AM"
Artwork by Andre Lamont Jackson
"JaMann Blessed It"

B.L.A.C.K.
Be Loving And Cee'k Knowledge

God, Goddess, King, Queen, Nubian, African,

Colored, Black, African-American, Ebony,

Brother, Sister, Earth, etc…

All original people no matter where we are from

we are ONE!

One blood,

One love,

One nation,

One heart,

And one consciousness.

So live your light,

Be the light,

Give the light,

And there shall be light on earth.

Black Girl In Italy

The girl with dimples and curls

Skin of bronze like the founder of faith

In …

Italy!

The land of lovers and sweet talkers

Olive oil and pasta

Paintings and sculptures

Villas and gangsters

But the pleasure is all theirs.

Your beauty illuminates any country!

MIND YOUR MOUTH

Because what goes around
Really goes around!

Proverbs: 18:8

Most of us will "lend an ear" to a succulent piece of gossip. However, just like swine, what seems so tasty going down can be quite harmful, mentally damaging and can give us an upset stomach! When it comes to gossip none of it is good, make no exceptions for those whispers that we "just had to" pass on. There is no way we can explain away our foolishness in spreading tales about others, hurting feelings, destroying characters and reputations and ruining our own testimonies. So the next time you're offered a "choice morsel" of gossip, let it end at you. Trust me, you'd appreciate it if others had a similar reaction when a story about you made the rounds. Let the meal end here before it upsets more than a stomach!

Who Are You Calling Crazy?

When I say "You're Crazy," I'm not literally calling you insane! I'm usually saying you're daring, courageous, bold, blunt, outspoken or right in your approach! The crazy part of it is that, I will not call a real "crazy (insane)" person crazy! I guess this is why I shouldn't use "slang," it confuses people!

FORGIVENESS

Making amends to fractured relationships is very difficult to do when the person you are trying to reconcile with doesn't meet you halfway. Express forgiveness and open your mind, heart and spirit to accepting forgiveness. It works both ways! And when the gift of forgiveness is offered: humbly accept it! This will begin the process of restoring relationships and making restitution to people we have wronged or may have wronged us. We should never be the one to withhold a pardon. Instead, extend the invitation of restoration to others humbly and without reservation.

ASIA

The woman is so named
In which the entire world was once called
As beautiful as the knowledge of all
I AM original

Do Your Homework

When you've done your consciousness homework, loved ones
You will have a clear spiritual psychology
And, hence, you will live in "the land of milk and honey"
And in never-ending "inner peace"

When you've done your consciousness homework, loved ones
You will have a happiness and harmony that surpasses understanding
And you will rest in the Father for evermore!

Lemons

Life gave 'em to me
So Imma make use of 'em
Aah … fresh ade!

Be Positive

Goals and aspirations are guiding forces throughout our lives.
When you find that hidden motivation inside of you, pull it out and be inspired.
Use your prayers to stay in touch with your inner strength.
Get out of your darkness by opening your eyes to the beauty that surrounds you.
Change your mood to positive and let your energy flow freely through your body.
Open your mind so you can think clearly to make wise decisions in all areas of your life.
My tale is told
My story is waiting to be heard
So you can learn from it
And make your story to be discovered.

Vohu Manah

Love yourself and all beings unconditionally
Love the Earth
Love nature
Love people and be a role model
Love animals and insects; they too have a purpose
Love culture
Live your spiritual ideas
Walk your talk
And practice what you lecture
For actions speak louder then words
And you will be on your way
To absolute peace
Embrace the Spenta Mainyu in you
And courageously realize your noble destiny
And fully realize
The great soul that you truly are!

Tonka

I pray that peace be within you.

Peace in your thoughts,

Peace in your words,

Peace in your feelings,

Peace in all your seeds,

Peace in your relationships,

Peace in your home,

Peace in your career,

Peace in your truths

And

Peace in your world because you are peace unto this world.

May peace, love and joy always be with (in) you.

Travion M. McGowan

Picture taken June 2012
On the Queen Mary Cruise Ship

To Know His Music Is To Know Him

His music is just as beautiful as his heart

They coincide

In the rhythm is where

The secret to his heart lies

Each beat glides and defines

What he holds inside

His lyrics compel my mind

In a very beautiful way

His music

His heart

What an amorous combination

So lovely together

11·26

Born day!

Happy Anniversary to the day you saw the light and became the light. May you continue to inspire and shine your rays of love and light on us. May peace always be with (in) you! I Love you Tonka!

The Sacred Trinity

Mind • Body • Spirit

Permits life on earth

Without even one of these three

We couldn't function properly!

Remain In Faith

Feeling the burden of numerous expectations
We may find it exhausting to be a model for others
I urge you not to quit "giving of yourself"
As we grow spiritually
The responsibility to help others will always be there
But the power to do so must always be genuine
And come from within

When Situations Arise

Focus on the positive

And view it as a learning experience

And you will move forward in peace

It's Sort Of Funny Yet Kind Of Sad

Up bright and early these familiar faces

Preparing for their daily races

Some going somewhere

Others going nowhere

Focus, focus, too focused on their focus

And it's sort of funny

Yet kind of sad

That the familiar faces

Never stop to ask

Who they are or who you are

Robotic, robotic, oh so programmed

What an abnormal world we live in

Stop The Violence

This black 'on' black violence doesn't earn you the stripes you really deserve; what it does is stunts our population, our growth, our awareness and our true purpose for our existence. If we continue to use retaliation, blame and ignorance as our reasons, guides, excuses and denials for our actions, we will self- destruct! I urge you to seek "knowledge of self" and to channel that same magnetic energy toward building and uniting, and by passing that awareness and knowledge to our youth. Only then will we grow as a unit and gain the real stripes, respect and leadership; it is our birthright. We are civilized and good by nature. It's time that you know it and show it. United we stand; divided we fall.

This Indian Girl

She found her way to L.A.

Attened college for five years here

And earned her B.A.

She still has an accent

A 24-karat gold nose ring

And her hair covered by a silk scarf

She hasn't lost her culture

And now here she is

Sitting next to me

Talking about her clothing business

While we sit and wait for our sellers permit

In Van Nuys, California

At the State Board of Equalization

All Season Long

I love him in the spring
Our season of growth
When all is renewed and green

I love him in the summer
Our season of warmth
When the sky is oh so blue

I love him in the autumn
Our season of sensation
When the breeze causes the leaves
To dance with the wind

I love him in the winter
Our season of calm and stillness
When the rain is falling down
Our love rises

Let's Plant Them Then Watch Them Grow

I like my flowers alive and vibrant rather than cut and dying. Therefore, if you are thinking of sending me flowers, I thank you, however, seeds will do and you planting them and watching them grow with me is even better!

Triumphant Thursday

When we try to crunch everything in so our Friday is free-flowing but don't stress the day! Today it's not about the people of success; it's about the people of value! Busy-bees, let's give something other then criticism, negativity and comparison. Show someone the importance they hold in your life whether it's to your work, personal or family life. Get creative and show them your flavor!

Be Accountable

Bring "passing the buck" to a halt

And accept responsibility for your own thoughts

and actions

Pointing the finger

Only pushes you further away

From the solution

When you accept responsibility

The resolution comes easily

Obstacles are just life lessons

Learn from your error

Correct it and move on

Do It For Yourself

Love astronomically and hate nothing
Make universal good your aim
All joys are yours if you put forth your claim
Spiritual laws shouldn't be misunderstood
Leave us with something that will aid us all
A word of encouragement, or a thought of excellent health
Whatever it is – Don't just do it for us
Also do it for yourself!

Eureka

The peace you search for is in the stillness of your heart.
The connection is with(in) the core of your essence.
When you dare to love unconditionally.
When you embrace love for love's sake,
You will come across peace.
The sense of freedom is invigorating.

Zaggin

They called us ... niggaz.
Now it is what we call ourselves.
We were whipped, hanged, raped and beat
And died for less than protesting to be free.
We were accused and abused and arrested
For merely sitting in the wrong seat
With fatigue and sore feet.
We were gunned down
For being black and proud
By those that called us ... niggaz.

They called us ... niggaz.
Now it is what we call ourselves.
Back when families were divided
And blood and sweat was shed on plantations
They called us ... niggaz.
Back when our lives, names, language, liberty, legacy, diet, land, clothes, religion, customs, traditions, identity, and dignity were taken
They called us ... niggaz.
Back when we cooked and cleaned and nursed and nurtured their children

They called us … niggaz.
Back when we built their homes and tailored their clothes
They called us … niggaz.
Back when we fought for our country as Buffalo Soldiers
They called us … niggaz.
Back when we were humiliated, bought and sold by those that called us … niggaz.

They called us … niggaz.
Now it is what we call ourselves.
The word shares the same stench no matter how skillfully we decide to use it.
We cannot masquerade hatred behind a term of endearment.
I urge you to embrace the positive names and titles that describe our true entity.
Royalty … just knowledge your history.
We have awakened from that sleep
We are reborn.
We are the Phoenixes that have risen from the ashes of those they called … niggaz.

Humility

Reverence of God

So Simple Then

I remember when all it took
Were a smile, a wink and a look.

Thousand Oaks Morning

Awakened by the singing of various birds outside my window. In unison they whistle and sing a song of glory. As I lie in bed trying to relate the tone to the type of bird, comes forth an image urging me to see the birds, so I get up and open my window and balcony door. I witness sparrows, crows, a hummingbird, a blue jay and those little brown birds are all flying around doing different things. The sparrows in the trees; the crows on the wire line; the hummingbird in a speedy motion flying to each shrub and tree eating the flower's nectar, the blue jay flying from tree to tree and there - are plenty of trees! And the little brown birds are also flying from tree to tree but in a group of three as if they're playing a game of tag. Yes, they are all doing their on thing. Yet, in harmony, they sing a melody so beautiful that it wakes me in calmness and allure.

The Bigger Person

There is so much power in an apology; followed by positive and honest reasoning.

Today, no blaming, no complaining nor asking someone to do something, that you would not do for them! Take ownership of your actions and how it may affect others; passing the buck is so uncivilized!

Reflection

So much has happened over the past years.
I have learned from both gains and losses,
Still, on some days,
I feel like my life is really just beginning,
And in some ways it is,
For though I have lived many years,
I never really knew love nor beauty entirely.
I thought love was selective and reserved for family, friends, and those who I choose to love. Until I met love and discovered we are one and the same and we have neither a status quo nor limitations to whom, how or what we love. I have enough love to love everyone and everything and I am fortunate to have been loved in return.

.

Enlighteners

I appreciate those that help others, especially when they do not know them, have never met them or may not ever meet them. Yet, when asked they give time, knowledge, or support. It's people like you that make me want to seek higher knowledge, wisdom and understanding. Everyone that responds out of love, helps to spread love, peace and happiness.

Yes It Is

The upside is knowing you love me more the morning after we've made beautiful music. After seeing all of my imperfections and still seeing me as a flawless beauty. The magic is real and make no mistakes about it, the feeling is mutual!

Worth A Thousand Words

Pictures turn into names, names turn into words, words turn into stories, stories can turn into rumors and rumors can turn into a misrepresentation of your character. So, the next time someone ask you for a picture, show consciousness in how you pose!

It Is The Best Policy

People fib, twist words and deceive out of panic. They worry that people will judge them harshly. Our love, trust, loyalty and friendship are given freely and openly.

Do not rob us of the truth; if you do, you rob yourself of a true and real response or reaction, which causes fake bonds to develop. Once the truth is exposed (and it will be at some point), you lose trust with that person; once trust is lost, so will be the relationship! To the deceivers: Increase your knowledge, love yourself, release your fears, lose your blame game, end your pity party, stop playing the victim. Enough with your excuses and reasons, own up to your responsibility, and straighten up and fly right! Why allow someone to believe something about you that is not true? To look good or accomplished in their eyes? Knock it off!

Bid Farewell

Hostility toward a person or thing
May feed the negative energy they need to persist.
So let's bid a loving farewell to the structures and agreements that no longer serves us.
Let's bid a caring farewell to ideas of inferiority, biases, prejudices and superiority.
While maintaining the gifts of wisdom,
Let's bid a kind farewell to tyranny and terrorism.
Let's bid a warm farewell to debt, score keeping and any economic structure that calls us to put making a living before living our lives to the absolute fullest!

The Human Brain

Designed to receive, process and transmit
Absolute truth!

CLARITY

I sit bare at the center of where

The four corners of the Earth meet

Not stripped of clothing

But of fear

No longer do I fear

So I sit with optimism and a clear understanding

of who I am

Why I am here and why the past of my ancestors

Speak to me

Like the marching sounds you hear

When you put a seashell to your ear

The voice is just as clear

So I listen

I take heed

And with the strength of their sacrifices

I will not live my life in vain

Elemental Love

If we're talking about where you send me
Have u heard of paradise?
This high I'm on 'cause of you
Feels nice.
Your eyes they spark, they bubble;
Going to get you in a whole lot of trouble;
What a little moonlight can do;
Can do to you when you're in love.
I'm a rare passionate fruit,
With inspiration from my roots.
I'm a tree with love on my leaves
And I choose you
To take a bite of my granadilla
So meet me at my villa
And bring with you
A bottle of "De Trafford Merlot"
What happens next
Only God knows
So let it unfold
Natural
You're a Lord

So of course

You send me metaphors

That's out of this universe

I am one with Mother Nature

So call me your Earth.

EARTH

Weighing in at 6 sextillion tons

From the land upon which the Sun first rose

Deeply rooted in nature

The bodies within her body are the vital building blocks of life

She is the main vein to the cycle of life

The reflection to the Sun

Mother to the stars and civilization

Sister to the trees and all elements

Love is her nourishment

With (In) You

If you are not doing your part to wake up humanity, to bring peace, forgiveness, knowledge, wisdom, understanding, equality and solutions. Then you are a part of the problem. It's time for you to wake up and listen from within. God doesn't need validation. God is all and in all. How you see the world is how you feel internally and therefore you will be affected. Remove all judgment and be that which you desire to have, and that's peace. God is love and so are you, but you got to wake up! Work on you instead of trying to change everybody else. The problem and solution is with (in) you.

Come Build With The Queen That Acknowledges You As King

I don't have a problem restoring something that I find to be valuable, classy and worth my time and effort
At renewing things, I am an expert
A good judge of character
I can tell you've been hurt
I'm counting on time
Time when you feel you've been healed
And can move forward.

Come build with the Queen that acknowledges you as King.
There's no feeling better
Than the joy you bring
You make my heart sing
And there is no denying the energy you bring.

Come build with the Queen that acknowledges you as King.
I'll follow your lead

Scholar, man of honor and virtue

Let's pursue the road of happiness together

For every second that passes, your past becomes more distant

I will not give up on you or us

Love, I'm persistent and consistent

I vow to always be there

Because I do care

And something as valuable, classy and worth my time and effort as you are

Is worth me putting in over-time to mend

I won't walk away and pretend this is our end because we chose each other and this is where our memories of love begins

I'm waiting on you to open up and let me in.

Come build with the Queen that acknowledges you as King.

GRATITUDE

Thankfulness and Appreciation

Get Thee Behind Me

The Gouger will continuously wrestle with our true nature,
Consistently trying to get us to give in to their way of thinking, eating and living,
Endlessly trying to keep us deaf, dumb and blind,
Again and again, trying to get us to be attracted to their temptations.
Once we recognize this,
We will obtain the strength
To terminate that influence once-and-for-all!

Gouger: a person who swindles you by means of deception or fraud.

What Once Was Will Be

It's pure ignorance to not be culturally attentive. It binds you to hide behind what blinded you in the first place. Without knowledge of other cultures, all you have to go by are the fabrications you were told, and with that ignorance you judge, stereotype and point the finger. But who's the real ignoramus? The people casting blame to cover their own shame? Not only do they not know your name, but also they have no knowledge of whence you came. No wonder you feel trapped; you've locked yourself in a box without any room to stretch! So you know how that goes: no room for growth. For your own personal growth and development, make yourself aware of whom you're sharing this earthly space with. And it is not with the ignorant. It is with the brilliant, the magnificent, supreme and gifted god-men and holy-women. Our story is the best and the worst in history - perfect symmetry and from the beginning of life in this realm, we are still here advancing the existence of humanity.

A Soul Mate Encounter

He was already a prominent thought in my mind.
When we met
I instantly knew the light in his eyes
A spark that almost blinded me.
I've been touched by the rays of
My soul mate.

The feeling was more like
A familiarity returning
A vibration re-occurring
Seeing each other
Re-activated our akashic memory
To who we are to ourselves, who we are to each other and why we are here.
In this moment
In this time
Our destiny became clear
Concurrently
And we both experienced
An awakening.

He Makes Time

Early morning

He calls to share his poetry with me

He wills me peace

Mid-day

He calls and asks how I am

And how my day is going

Late night

He wills me a good night

His voice …

The last sound I hear before I sleep

Carefully Chosen Words

Thinking before speaking is wisdom. We need to weigh the impact of our words. We don't want to tell a confidence to the biggest blabbermouth in town, even if that person is nice and may have shared things in confidence with us. Nor do we want to hurt the feelings of others. Unwise words will reveal that we are not living in wisdom and can land us in uncompromising positions. Thinking before speaking will save us a lot of trouble and heartache. So to keep our souls clean and to keep from doing wrong with our words, speak wisely and truthfully.

Who's Counting?

I envision life without timepieces,
without calendars,
without these constant reminders that
we're either early or we're running late
or we're running out of time … to live.

I Want To

I want to blow into your ears
and rub my fingers through your hair
I want to hear you through your silence and
know what you have not said
I want to read you like a poem then write poems
inspired by you
I want to have fun under the sun then have wine
and dine with you
I want to be okay when you are away
Because I know, you will return soon
I want to unwind with a kiss of your lips
I do not want make sense
I want to make mistakes, make up, make out and
make love with you
Because, that is, what two people in love, do.

Stepping Stone

We met in a challenging world

During troubling times

Built on untruths

Held down by fears

Drenched in consequence

Yet, sheltered with love, a will and a spark of optimism

We used those milestones as stepping-stones

And our love grew through a world of stone

Reflections Of True Self

I follow a path to understand

The lessons of life

I learn much from every experience

In old and new experiences

In gaining and earning

During many challenges

In giving service and support to others …

I learn Self

Understanding Self goes beyond thought

Self dwells in a timeless place

My connecter that is in silence yet speaks to me

in a still and small voice

All is a reflection of all within

7

He walks in divinely like the luminous

And starlit sky at night

And all that is best of dark

Embark in his walk

He is that star that sparkle

Brighter than the others

Guiding me to walk in his direction

Tales Of An Urban Sufi

As I traveled through the pages of his book
I got a glimpse into his heart and mind
I find him to be virtuous, creative and inspiring
He is not average … He is original
He is an Urban Sufi!

Respect

If you respect yourself everyone else will follow. You can only disrespect yourself when your only option to gain respect is through harsh words, intimidations or inconsiderate actions. Men be the type of men you want your daughters to marry and the type of men you want your sons to be. God is love, show it and you will be loved and respected in return!

No Rush

There isn't a timeline on being honest but there is a timeline on what we share!

Orange Arie

My sweet mother

Whose face wears the moments

Of my childhood years

I love you and thank you with all of my heart

For always being there.

BABIES

Babies are precious

Take care of your babies

Love them

Tell them that you love them

Hug them

Kiss Them

Teach them

Guide them

Include them

And

Show them that life is to be lived

SPLENDIFEROUS SUNDAY

Today, no blaming nor complaining! Where there is blame, you are sure to find shame of irresponsibility. Taking ownership brings you one step closer to peace within. We are meant to be at peace with ourselves as well as amongst others.

SET THE EXAMPLE

We should not allow the devil to trick us into mimicking his nature. So, let's not lose control of what we are able to control, which is ourselves, our temperament, our actions and the love for each other. We have to exercise patience with our family members because some people, as you know, don't understand themselves; they are lost and unaware. Here is where we need our strength to stay above the petty, but not stray from our duty; you know the saying: Each one, teach one. When people begin to see that their harsh words don't upset your spirit, they will seek help from you because they will see your strength and want some of it! Knowledge of ourselves and proper communication, understanding, wisdom, patience, forgiveness and love for one another, unity, mercy and grace is my prayer for us all.

Surmount

I derive from the greatness

Of great men and women

That survived a holocaust and overcame

systematic oppression

And became the symbol of positive progression

Our ancestors remained unified during

segregation

And remained spiritual wealthy during inflation

They stayed strong in the storm during the reign

of an abusive nation

Their tale is told so that we may grow

And use their strength and sacrifice as an anchor

to surmount

Happiness Is Here

Happiness is here
All the while
You can feel it in my words
See it in my smile
Hear it in my voice
Every moment we spend conversing
Touch my life and my soul
The things that we share and learn
Adds permanent growth that we've earned.

The changes I see
And what I have learned about me
What I have learned about you
What you have learned about yourself
And what you have learned about me
are a response to how we live our lives
and what we discover in each other.

No matter what the future holds
No matter what we are told.
We are connected by our souls

Our time might be different a year from now
But we are part of each other forever
That much is certain.

Enjoying The Tweets And Tapping Sounds

Enjoying the chirps and songs of many birds. Standing on my balcony I could see a couple crows (they're so huge maybe they're ravens), ducks (flying), hummingbirds, sparrows and (are you ready) a woodpecker! This little guy is so cute but super-noisy!

The Deadliest Weapon

A Queen knows the power of her tongue
And she will never use it as a weapon toward her King.
She knows that speaking without thinking
Is a dangerous thing.
Wisdom is grand!

Submission Takes Humility!

A submissive wife voluntarily follows her husband's leadership; it is not forced on her! Submission doesn't mean she is weak!

A submissive wife doesn't nag, deceive or manipulate. She understands that this behavior disturbs nature's design of partnership roles.

A submissive wife must first learn to trust her husband's goodness and his dominion.
This doesn't mean she sit-by while her husband makes all the family decisions. In a healthy relationship, they work as a team. When a decision cannot be agreed upon, the leader makes it, knowing he is responsible foremost for that decision.

A submissive wife also offers effective communication, support and encouragement because she understands that making decisions is a heavy responsibility on a man's shoulders.

Casual Sex

There is nothing casual about sex.

Sex without a connection and without love is a meaningless experience.

Sex (love-making) is at the root of life and has to be understood fully to experience it.

True sex never fails, as it is a bond between two people that have come together. Therefore, sex can be termed as an art in itself. A kind of act that is good when properly performed but to enjoy it thoroughly, it also needs the unity of the mind, heart and soul. Sex is not just an act of pleasure but also the feeling of togetherness, being so close to another person and being comfortable in the union.

ASIA

A woman of wisdom

Strength and virtue

Inner beauty

Alluring and Awesome

(I wrote this while teaching elementary students how to write acrostic poems using their names)

Forgive Me

Forgive me for

The things that, I never said to you.

Forgive me for

Not expressing my gratitude.

Forgive me for

Not showing how much I appreciated you.

Your love was felt in multitudes.

Kiss

Kiss and tell
I don't have to say a word
My kiss tells my story

The Shape Of Beauty

Is looking into the dreamy eyes
Of the woman
That wants to be understood
In a way that only the man
Kissing her can understand
And comprehend ... Her Love

The shape of beauty
Is feeling electricity in the touch
Of the woman
That wants to not only feel his skin
But touch his soul
And with understanding
He protects and holds ... Her Love

The shape of beauty
Is understanding her attempt to speak words
That are a fraction as good as his kiss
He listens
He guides
And discerns ... Her love

Low Clouds

Los Angeles during this time of year
One should always bring an umbrella
When you leave the hills
Rain often falls on the city
This is because the clouds are so low

Messy People

A messy person is one that instigates trouble for the sake of keeping people in an ignorant state of mind (misery-loves -company sort of way). Most messy people that I know are of low esteem and need to keep the climate at a degree that they can comprehend so that they can remain a part of the atmosphere / environment / conversation. Because in truth, fairness and in intelligent conversations or atmospheres, they simply can't keep up! So to keep people from recognizing their ignorance, they just use tactics to draw others into their ill-mannered cloud! They lack love, appreciation, consideration and care. The sad thing is most messy people don't know they are messy because it comes natural to them, like survival skills!

BRAGGART

When it comes to people speaking on their "good deeds," I have mixed thoughts. On one hand, I think it's good to share what you've done for people with others (not everyone you meet) because your story may inspire others to do selfless and noble deeds as well. We are to be examples for others. On the other hand, a person that just talks to get a pat on the back (braggart) is unbecoming!

Read More

During the L.A. riots

Clothing, food, appliance, electronics,

Jewelry and gun stores

Were looted

But not one bookstore!

Oak Trees

What I know about Oak trees:

They are of great strength and hardness

And Oak wood makes fine furniture.

They are distinctive and attractive trees.

It was said that Jacob buried the gods of his people under an Oak tree.

I know that some people use Oak in winemaking, it's said to add many different dimensions by providing flavor and fragrant support to wine.

I also know that they produce acorns and squirrels love them for it!

Autumn

The leaves dance in the streets
To the rhythm of the wind

Eden

When a woman loves a man

She walks with him

Hand in hand

In a garden

Where all is theirs to embrace

The fragrance

The scenery

The sound

Of nature is there for them to enjoy

And apples fall from knowledge trees

Freely for them to eat

Pathfinder

May the ancient scrolls guide my footsteps

During my quest for the rarest jewel

My shadow dance

Like gypsies around a bonfire

And once again my soul takes to the journey

To find his eyes

Who actually see

What is at reach

So near

The face of God awaits

Better Than They Imagine

By the grace of God

She will be better than they imagine

Physical attraction

Without attraction to the inner

Is like eating unclean food.

Honor the queen

That stepped out of your dream

For she knows respect, patience and love

She always speak the truth

She is someone you can trust

In you she is a believer

Her beauty grows from modesty

Not by displaying her features.

Let's live this lifetime

Comparison to the next

Her wisdom reflects

That she knowledge God is wise

Her words are always kind

Her beauty grows from within

She has a special connection to creation

For she is

The mother to nature, tribes and all nations
She trusts your revelations
And her faith.
By the grace of God
She will be better than they imagine.

Visions

Your visions are what bring your reality into fruition and as this fruit becomes ripe, ready to fall and plant the seeds of a new future, remember, you are here to become, feel and know all rhythms of all life as well as your soul's rhythm, then harmony

Sharing Is Caring

I saw another side of him.

Displaying no caution he was unguarded and completely opened as I was and as our spirits danced into the night, he held me tight. He spoke from his heart and shared.

Communication

A must to sustain a healthy relationship. Proper communication is being honest, respectful, open, and non-threatening. When you truly love someone, you will always know what to say and how to treat them.

Evermore

From the warmth of the wind
I knew love surely hath been breathing here
The zephyr says he is near
No voice as yet made the air
But the sense of promise is everywhere.

Then like the wind he appeared
He was a dream remembered in a dream
The sound of his voice
Put other voices to sleep
The breeze hummed love evermore.

Beauty

I've traveled to many places and have seen

Colors and beauty in many forms

I've seen and been in the presence of:

Natural beauty

Pure beauty

Innocent beauty

Exaggerated beauty

Exotic beauty

Beauty in cultures

Beauty in accents

But my heart hankers for

Someone that possess

Inner beauty and spoken beauty

To share my life with

Because out of all the beauty in the world

Inner beauty never fades

Uplift

I find it startling how one word, one mood or one vibe can change a person's opinion on who you are. I strive to empower and inspire others and I will the people in my realm will do the same when I need to be elated!

Fifth Commandment

I love and honor my parents and just when I think I am teaching them something, they drop some facts on me and open my eyes! Sometimes when you think your protecting them – it's them that are protecting you. Honor and respect your Mother and Father and you will live long and blessed.

Poetry To Me

Poetry to me is an incredible gift

An elusive language that helps shape the way we

feel as well as the way, in which we connect,

define and linger with our memories.

Poetry has the power to unlock the doors we tend

to push shut with the business of every day life.

Stearns Wharf

The sun shines and the wind blows on and past me
Enjoying the Emerald Tablet
As I drive
To the city where the beach calls out to me
Storks flying over me
Artists displaying their art on the Wharf
The pier has no rails
But it does have coin-op binoculars
And saloons with free wine tasting
It's clean and refreshing here
As I walk along the shore
I see a couple parasailing
It must be nice to have someone to do that with
Then the likkle youths ask me to join them in kite-flying
Then Frisbee
I wondered what made them ask me
A stranger to them
We played and it was peace
I returned to my stroll

Until I found my place on the sand
As I sit and sip on this piña colada
And grab my favorite pen
That I still can't believe hasn't been stolen yet
I write
And strive to describe the peace I'm feeling
As I drive back to the Oaks
Listening to this Mad World
I recognize life is good!

Maximal

Us together make heaven here on Earth
We know the use of knowledge and wisdom's worth
And understand the importance of our people's rebirth
With culture and a free-dome we can abolish mental restraints
Then refine our creative power of being equal with all in existence
As God intended
We are here to build not destroy
To elevate and to add-on positive energy to our nation
We are born complete.

Giver Of Kingship

He has the voice of an ancient and triumphant song

When you hear his astuteness

You see peace

You feel love

You hear inspiration

And you taste fulfillment

His laugh is as a transverse wave transferring energy

His strength intensified our ecstasy

And our love glowed like a coal

In the center of the furnace

As he knew me and named me

His Queen

Magnificent Yellow

Our love grows and blossoms
Affably as orchids
In the purest hope of summer
My heart follows your kora voice
And leaps like a serval
At the whisper of your name
The night floats in on a great eagle wing
I am comforted by your handkerchief
That I carry into the
Twilight of existence beams
And hold next to my cheek
As my gown falls from my shoulders
It reminds me of your instrument
In the quiet
I listen for the last chime of the day
I wait in the moonlight
For your secret interest
So that we may love as one
Jointly
In search of magnificent yellow and mystical
love

Birds

All living species of birds have wings

They can do what we can only do in spirit, and that is fly

They soar and sing ... tweedle-dee-dee

And they have perfect eyesight and balance.

I love birds they're pretty,

They add life to the sky

And I take nothing away from flightless birds

Because they have wings yet can not actually fly

But like us they add beauty to the land

And to the balance of "as in heaven, so on Earth!"

Power Of Poetry

I believe poetry has the power to enter us and open ideas and imagery inside of us so indiscernibly, so circumstantially, that often we're not even aware that we are coming out of a great poem as a different person from the person we were when we began reading it.

I Write

I write serious lines, which may perhaps be of some spiritual advantage to your soul.

I write about truth and principles, which may perhaps be of some Influence upon the right ordering of which you need clarity.

I write about love, to love — to be loved and the scared bond of love, which may perhaps breed love in you.

I write about nature, which may perhaps open one's awareness to our connection.

I write on various topics for various reasons; most of all I write because I love to!

Perennial

Pace yourself, you'll get there

We are all traveling toward the light, on Jacobs-Ladder

Some of us are at the top

Some in the middle

Others on the bottom

It's our choice

Whether to take the long path or the short path

As long as we continue to rise upward

We will all reach the top!

ENCORE

(Poetry by Orange Arie)

Rain

Lord, send the rain
After the rain
Withered things are restored
And made green again
The flowers flourish and lend their
Fragrance to the air
Removing the stench of previous despair
Dreams are renewed
Hope is revived
And again we are determined
To give life our hardest try
The rain washes away pain
Allowing us to breathe again
After the rain the dark clouds disappear
And our minds are made miraculously clear
Lord, send the rain
We need the rain

By, Orange Arie

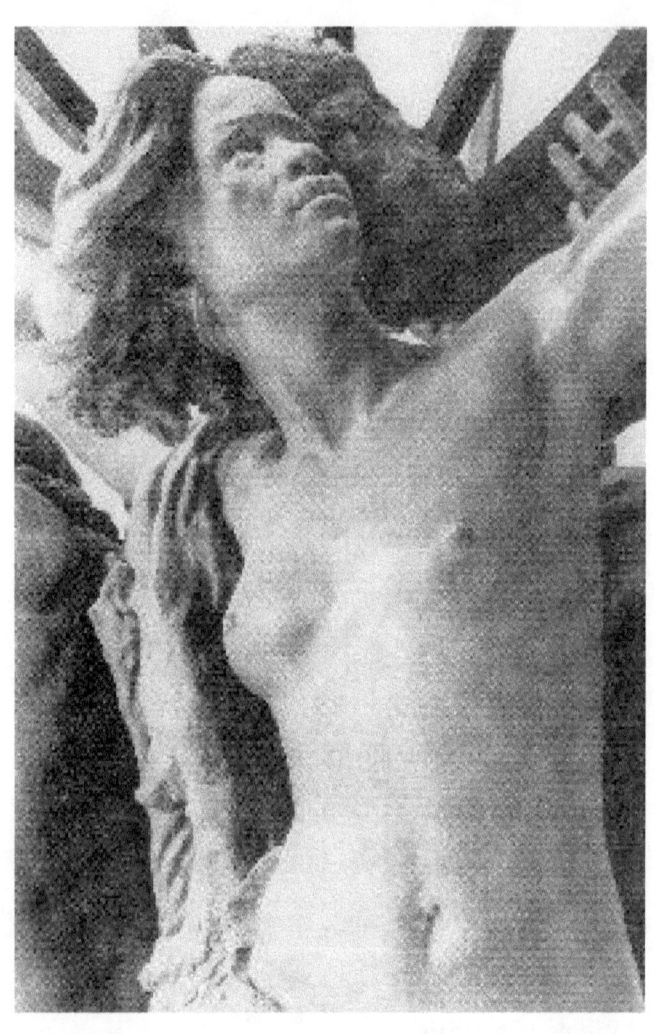

The "Fountain of the Observatory" sculpture by Jean-Baptiste Carpeaux.
This picture is of "Africa" one of the four figures of the sculpture
Located in Paris, France

Black Mother

Black Mother, Black Mother
I see you in your kitchen
Oven on
Dishwasher hot
Mop bucket full
Washing machine wringing
And you are walking around singing
You are such a busy bee!
If anyone should ask why
What would be your reply?
I would just say
I'm acting as the maid
Until the maid shows up
And she has not showed up in forty years
And I'm only forty-two

Black Mother, Black Mother
You're walking down the street
At 7:30 a.m. in the morning
With four little children
As happy as can be
Their coats look new
And their boots do too
But your dress seems rather worn

And your sweater is wearing thin
Why are you out so early
In this cold and gusty wind?
I'm walking my children to school
My car broke down a year ago
And these streets are dangerous, you know
So right now
I'm their security
Until they're old enough to know

Black Mother, Black Mother
I see you in a home
But for some unknown reason
The address is not your own
Furniture polish beside you
Dutch cleanser in one hand
And glass cleaner in the other
Can you give me an explanation
For all of this Black Mother?
Well daughters need shoes
Sons want a bike
I'm a little late with the rent
And the landlord can be such a fright
Since I cannot accept defeat
I'm just being the one that make ends meet

Black Mother, Black Mother
Such a touching sight I see
There's a beautiful black child
With her head upon your knee
Your words are spoken softly
As you stroke her long black hair
Will you tell me the reason her head is there?
My child has a problem
As children often do
But I'm not the type of mother
Who cries "Oh what am I to do?"
So I quickly turn myself into a sponge
That absorbs her growing pains
Her disappointments and her tears
In return I give encouragement
That will last throughout her years
Black Mother, Black Mother
Where are you rushing to?
Your eyes are sad
Your face is tight
Your hands are sweating so
Tell me Black Mother quickly
Where is this place you go?
I'm going to see my son
He's serving time, you know
He had to learn the hard way

Being in the wrong place
At the wrong time
And doing the wrong thing
Will send you to places
You never intended to go
So you see this day is rather new to me
Because today I'm something
I'd thought I'd never be
A visitor with a time limit
Between my child and me

Black Mother, Black Mother
You stand so proud today
With a sparkle in your eyes
A smile kissed by the sun
And your giving words of encouragement
To each and everyone
Being an observer of all the things you do
I can't help but wonder
What has caused this reaction in you?
My girls are all grown up now
With good jobs and families of their own
They let my son come out that iron gate
The Lord blessed him with a good mind
And now he's living straight
He's at the right place

At the right time
Doing the right thing
And that would cause
Any mother's heart to sing

Black Mother, Black Mother
You're full of years by now
Your eyes are dim, your hair is thin
And your steps are getting slow
But there is one more question
I need to ask and then I'll let you go
Through all these years you have been
Strength, hope and encouragement
To everyone you know
Now I would like to know the source
That caused all these virtues inside of you to grow?
Oh shucks that's easy
I could have answered that question
A long, long time ago
You see I am God's prize possession
And it is He that has made me so

BY, ORANGE ARIE

God Made Me Free

When God made the oceans and the seas
He gave them boundaries
So they would not over flood the earth
When God created me
He gave no boundaries
God made me free
Let it be ... let it be
God made the stars to illuminate the night
God made me also a very bright and shining light
But you pretend not to see
Stop and take a look at me
I am the representation
Of every dark skin person you will ever see
And God has placed such an excellent spirit
Inside of me
I shall exceed all limits
Given me by society
God placed me in a home
Where the air was clean to breath
Free from injustice, degradation and immorality
In my home all were free to enjoy life

The way God planned it to be

I was stolen from my home

The country of my birth

And forced to work for people that claimed

I had no worth

I've been whipped, I've been hung

I've been cheated, I've been chained

Yet of these things

I am not ashamed

Because it happened during my season of rain

But now the dark clouds have been

Rolled away

And for me it is a brand new day

Today I am a doctor, a lawyer

A judge, a schoolteacher, a business owner

And a presidential candidate

I am all the things I have ever hoped to be

Because God has given me the victory

God made me free

Let it be … let it be

BY, ORANGE ARIE

www.ingramcontent.com/pod-product-compliance
Lightning Source LLC
Chambersburg PA
CBHW021157160426
43194CB00007B/780